# mammalabilia

poems and paintings by

## Douglas Florian

voyager books · harcourt, inc.

ORLANDO · AUSTIN · NEW YORK · SAN DIEGO · TORONTO · LONDON

Thanks to Sue Nemeroff of Chorley School
for suggesting the phrase "one lump or two"
as regards the camel.

www.HarcourtBooks.com

First Voyager Books edition 2004
*Voyager Books* is a trademark of Harcourt, Inc., registered in
the United States of America and/or other jurisdictions.

The Library of Congress has cataloged the hardcover edition as follows:
Florian, Douglas.
Mammalabilia: poems and paintings/by Douglas Florian.
p.  cm.
Summary: A collection of humorous poems about mammals such as
the tiger, gorilla, and rhebok.
1. Mammals—Juvenile poetry.  2. Children's poetry, American.
[1. Mammals—Poetry.  2. American poetry.]  I. Title.
PS3556.L589M36    2000
811'.54—dc21    99-10702
ISBN 0-15-202167-1
ISBN 0-15-205024-8 pb

A C E G H F D B

# Contents

# The Aardvarks

Aardvarks aare odd.
Aardvarks aare staark.
Aardvarks look better
By faar in the daark.

# The Bactrian Camel

Mr. Bactrian, a question for you— about your back: one lump or two?

# The Fox

Clever.
Cunning.
Crafty.
Sly.
A fox composed this poem,
Not I.

# The Coyote

I prowl.
I growl.
My howl
Is throaty.
I love
A vowel,
For I am coyo$^{oo}$$^o$ote.

# The Gorilla

A gentle giant
Blessed with grace . . .

It's stilla
Gorilla—
Don't get in its face.

# The Beaver

Wood-chopper
Tree-dropper
Tail-flopper
Stream-stopper

# The Zebras

How many zebras
Do you see?
    I see two zebras.
I see three.
    I see three, too.
I see four.
    I see four, too.
I see more!

# The Lynx

Some people wear fur coats of lynx.
I
think
that
stynx.

# The Ibex

The daring ibex risk their necks
On scary, airy mountain treks.
Each one must climb with skill complex,
Or else become an **ex**-ibex.

24

# The Otter

I state most emphatic:
An otter's aquatic.
An otter loves water—
An utter fanatic.
It's most acrobatic,
And quite charismatic.
I state most emphatic:
An otter's aquatic.

# The Rhebok

The rhebok's main
Claim to fame
Is its name.

# The Elephant

An elephant, rising,
Finds grass appetizing.
And how it loves munchin'
More grass for its luncheon,
As well as its dinner.
It's not getting thinner
And not looking leaner—
It's just growing greener.

# The Mule

Voice of the mule: bray
Hue of the mule: bay
Fuel of the mule: hay
Rule of the mule: stay

# The Tapir

The shape of a tapir
Seems better on paper.

# The Lemurs

In Madagascar leaping lemurs breeze through trees without breaking femurs.

# The Giraffe

Rubber-necker
Double-decker
Cloud-checker
Star-trekker

# The Hippo

By day the hippo loves to float
On swamps and lakes, much like a boat.
At night from water it retreats,
And eats
      and eats
           and eats
                and eats.

# The Boar

The boar at best
Is just a pig
That wears a vest,
And coat, and wig.

# The Bear

Come Septem-bear
I sleep, I slum-bear,
Till winter lum-bears
Into spring.
More than that's
Em-bear-rassing.

# The Porcupine

The porcupine
Can climb up pine.
On bark and leaves
It loves to dine.
The porcupine
Has porcupins
That sprout out from
Its porcuskin,
And if you touch one,
You'll complain:
The porcupine's
A porcupain.

# The Tiger

I am a cat—come hear me purrrr.
I've many stripes upon my furrrr.
I speed through forests like a blurrrr.
I hunt at night—I am tigerrrr.

The illustrations in this book were done in gouache on primed brown paper bags.
The display type was set in Windsor Bold.
The text type was set in Sabon.
Color separations by Bright Arts Graphics Pte. Ltd., Singapore
Printed and bound by Tien Wah Press, Singapore
Production supervision by Sandra Grebenar and Pascha Gerlinger
Designed by Kaelin Chappell